The Little Tree

Saving Our Planet

Here is the pot.

Here is the soil.

Here is the little tree.

Look at the soil.

The soil goes in here.

The little tree
goes in here too.

Look at the water.

The water is for

the little tree.

The little tree

likes the water.

The little tree

likes the sun.

The little tree

goes up.

The little tree

goes up and up.

Look at the little tree.